Going to the Movies

Julie Haydon

Contents

Chapter 1	**Saturday**	2
Chapter 2	**The Movie Theater**	5
Chapter 3	**Screen Nine**	8
Chapter 4	**On the Big Screen**	13
Chapter 5	**Making a Movie**	18
Glossary and Index		24

Chapter 1: Saturday

I am staying at Uncle Brett's for the weekend.

Today Uncle Brett took me to see a movie.

First, we looked on the **Internet** to see what movies were playing.

Uncle Brett wanted to go
to the **local** movie theater.
A lot of movies for children were playing.
I picked one for us to see.

Chapter 2
The Movie Theater

We went to the movie theater.
We had to get in line to buy our tickets.

Uncle Brett let me buy some popcorn and a drink from the concessions stand.

NOW SHOWING

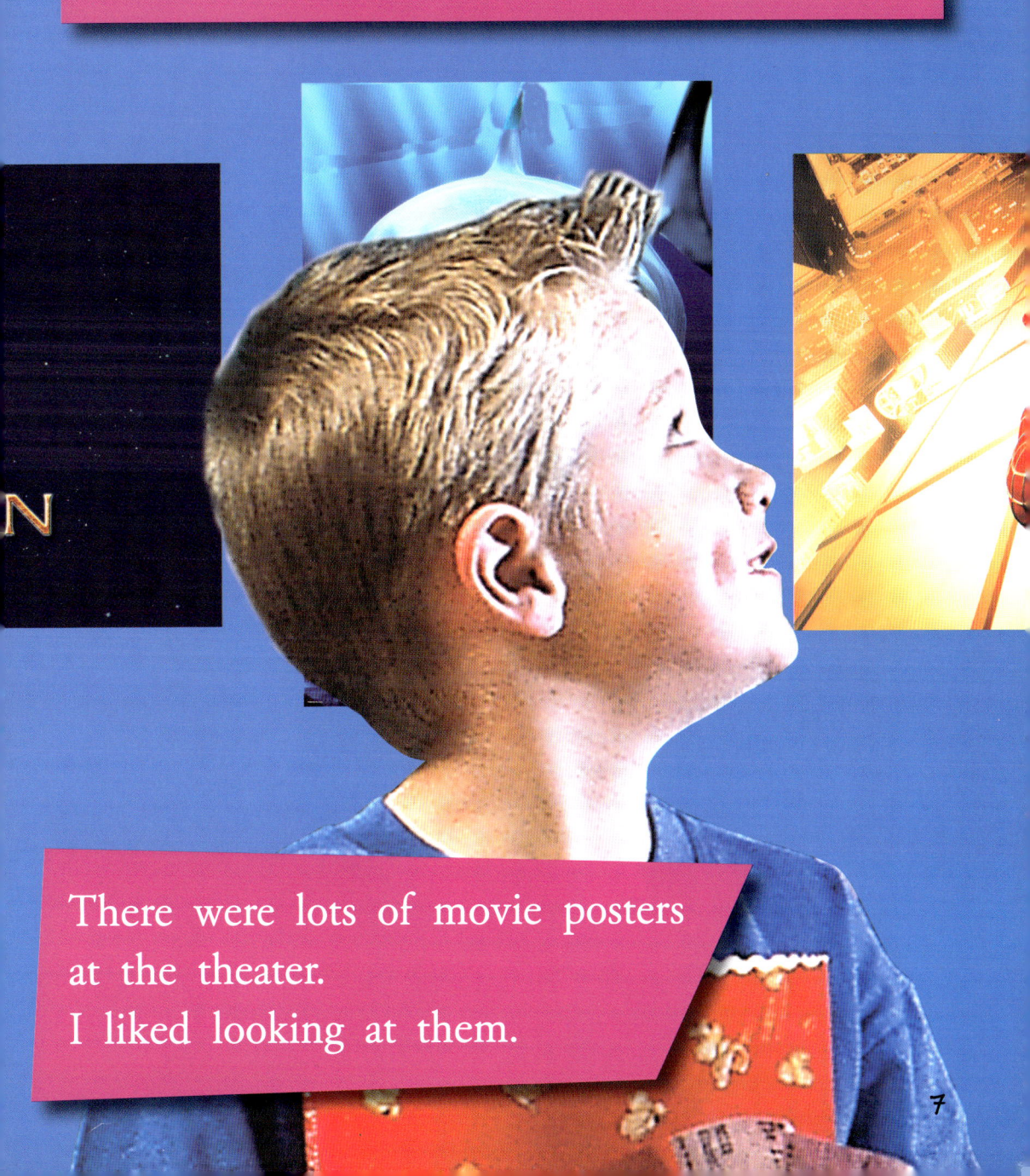

There were lots of movie posters at the theater.
I liked looking at them.

Chapter 3

Screen Nine

I gave our tickets to an **usher**.
He checked the tickets.
Then he tore them in half.
He gave us back our ticket **stubs**.

There were ten **screens** at the theater. Our movie was showing on screen nine.

The lights were on in the theater.
It was full of rows of seats.
There was a huge screen
at the front of the theater.

Uncle Brett and I sat down in our seats. Other people came in and sat down, too.

Then the lights slowly went off,
and music started playing.
Uncle Brett and I watched the screen.

Chapter 4: On the Big Screen

It was dark in the theater now. **Advertisements** started playing on the screen.

...Available in the lobby

13

Then the movie began.
It was loud and full of color.
The pictures on the screen moved quickly.
It was so exciting!

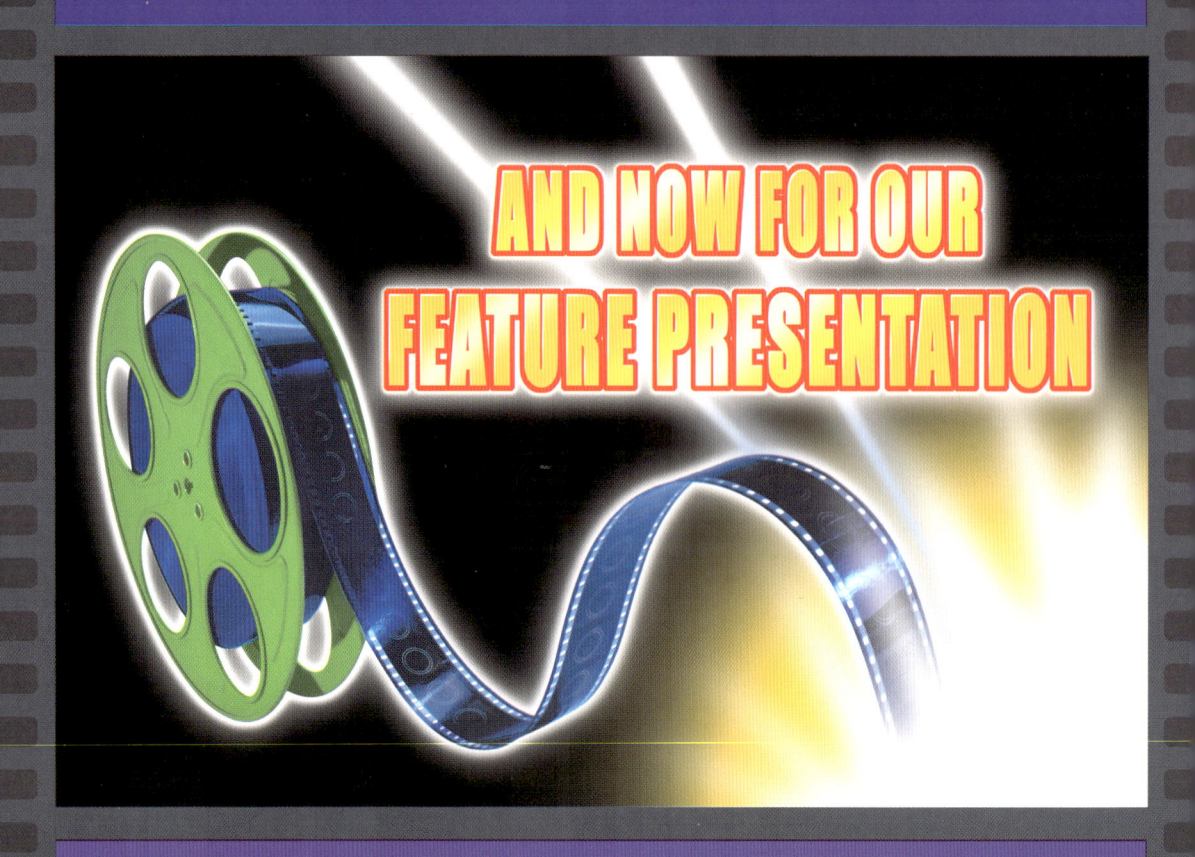

Names came up on the screen. They were some of the people who had made the movie. The name of the movie came up on the screen, too.

Directed by..............................Robert McCreight

Produced by.............................Karen Aroian

Story by...................................Tom Sjoerdsma

Screenplay by..........................Lee Walker

Cast of Characters

Peter..Rick Watson

Wendy......................................Jane Turpin

John...Alex Corona

Michael....................................Tim Posner

I watched the movie.
Sometimes it was funny.
Sometimes it was exciting.
Sometimes it was a little sad.
I was having great fun!

The movie ended ninety minutes later.
We left the theater and talked about the movie.

I thanked Uncle Brett for taking me
to the movies.
Then I asked him how movies are made.
What a day!

Chapter 5
Making a Movie

A writer writes the story, or **screenplay**. The screenplay has all the words that the actors will say in the movie.

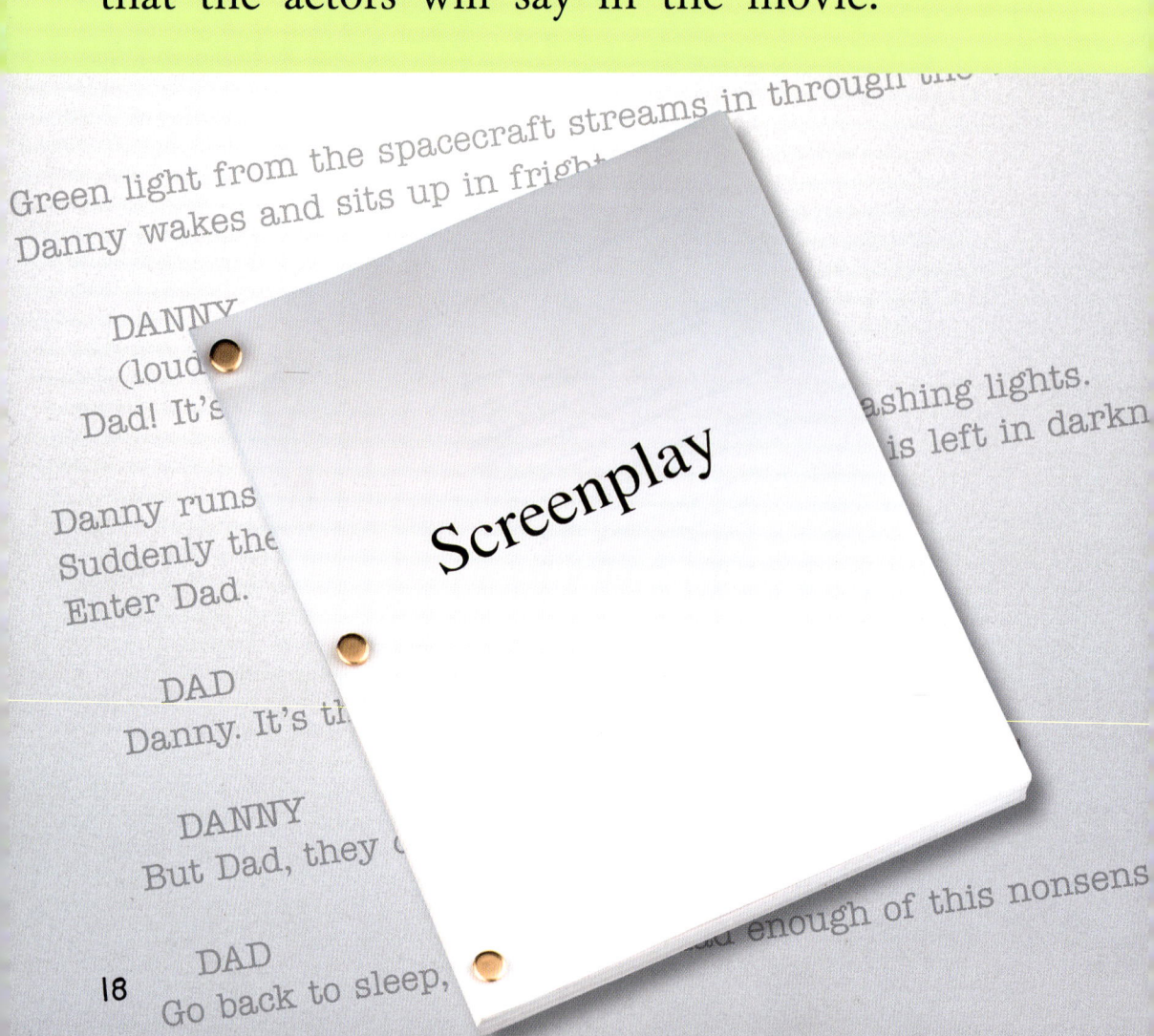

The person who tells everyone what to do while the movie is being made is the **director**.

Actors play the people in movies.
Some actors are very famous.

Naomi Watts

Orlando Bloom

20

Movies are made on film.
Lots of film is used.
A film **editor** puts the best parts
of film together to make the movie.

Lots of other people work on a movie, too.

There are people who:

* work the cameras
* work the lights
* make the **sets**

- get the sound right
- work on computers
- find or make clothes for the actors
- put makeup on the actors

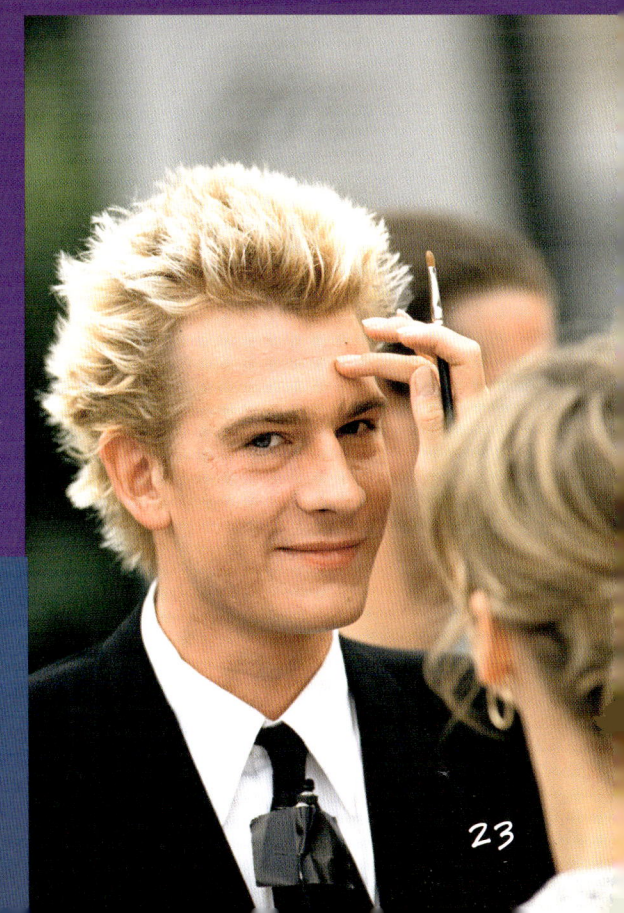

Glossary

advertisements   messages that tell people about things they can buy

director   a person who is the boss while a film is being made

editor   a person who puts parts of film together to make a movie

Internet   lots of computers that are linked together and share information

local   not far away

screen   a flat, white area on which movies are shown

screenplay   a written story for a movie

sets   furniture, buildings, and other things that are made for movies

stubs   leftover parts of tickets

usher   a person who works in a cinema or theater taking tickets and showing people to their seats

Index

actors   18, 20, 23
advertisements   13
cameras   22
clothes   23
computers   23
director   19
film editor   21
Internet   3
lights   10, 12, 22

makeup   23
screen   10, 12, 13, 14, 15
screenplay   18
sets   22
sound   23
story   18
tickets   5, 8
writer   18